Old

Basil du Toit

smith|doorstop

Published 2015 by
smith|doorstop Books
The Poetry Business
Bank Street Arts
32–40 Bank Street
Sheffield S1 2DS

Copyright © Basil du Toit 2015
All Rights Reserved

ISBN 978-1-910367-50-6
Typeset by Utter
Printed by People for Print, Sheffield

Acknowledgements
My thanks to the editors of the following publications,
in which some of these poems first appeared: *Carapace*,
Illuminations, *New Contrast*, *Poetry Review*, *Under the Radar*,
and the Shore Poets Anthology, *Such Strange Joy*.

smith|doorstop Books are a member of Inpress:
www.inpressbooks.co.uk. Distributed by Central Books Ltd.,
99 Wallis Road, London E9 5LN

The Poetry Business is an Arts Council
National Portfolio Organisation

Contents

5	Old
6	After The Dance
7	Shaman Songs For A Tsunami
8	The Nation Makers
9	Cooking Rice By The Delia Smith Method
10	Dog Dinners
11	Audience Coughing, Bayreuth 1951
12	Duzi Marathon
13	A Posthumous Dictation
14	Skin
15	Under Your Skin
16	Metatarsus Varies
17	Darwin's Music
18	Historic Computing Machines
19	1789
20	Sound Engineer
21	Powers Over There
22	Extinction Level Events
23	Isolation
24	The Fierce Wheat In Samuel Palmer
25	Labours Of Delight
26	Quiet Reading Room
27	Why I Am Not A Poet
28	The Daisy In My Wake
29	In A Hide

In memory of Ursula and Louis.

Old

There is surely a faint olfactory foreshadowing
of death in the bodies of the very old;
the organs inside are sweating with decay
and giving off that odour of confinement,
that fungal smell of furred strawberries
and things forgotten at the back of the fridge.

Old skin is going off, has gone bad,
and is blackening with cankers to that effect,
but that premonitory whiff of putrescence
comes from deep within the autumnal lapse
of this creature – it has started to turn,
to go sour on itself, to thicken in its liquids.

Only the driest and most minimal linen
can offset these tendencies (nothing can halt them)
and the most rationed and scrupulous diet
and constant bowel-rinsing in the Ganges
and a hard bed and the works of Milton
and a dry lifestyle, a very dry lifestyle.

After The Dance

My body is full of klezmer aches
from skips and knee bends, hops
and shuffles, stamps and turns.
Clarinets and fiddles play on
in me long after the musicians
have packed up and gone home.

My body is a plain church hall
whose floorboards have been stamped
all over for a good few hours
by homely Gentile/Jewish feet.
I can't switch off that keilidh –
I'm ringing with the aftershocks.

My hands recall the perfumes
of dozens of laughing women
whose waists I've hugged in dances.
Yiddish accordians send crazy
electric dazzles down both legs.
I'm still holding the ghosts of

fifty fragrant women in my arms.

Shaman Songs For A Tsunami

Something inevitable is coming after you, running
under its own steam, unerringly as a legal process.
You're trying to stay ahead of it, the advancing black
wall of debris the world's uneasiness has launched.
Earth clearing its throat sheered off a whole promontory
which slid storey after storey into the bulging sea,

and the rest is wave mechanics and open waters.
If you conceptualize fast enough you might not
get caught in the wash cycle of churning timber.
You can dance whatever slippery steps you like
to keep yourself buoyed above the gnashing rubble –
unfurl more sail, pocket more impelling breeze.

Fly on your chantings, on your airborne incantations,
keep the thin language buffer going between you
and the rushing, rely on that linguistic air cushion,
that seal of breath separating impacts; voice your
evacuation from the shambles, from the whirling blades
of plank and girder trying to crush you like a songbird.

The Nation Makers

Even now, men in kilts
in bald, Hebridean places
are stirring up history
in marginal languages.

Men in full folk garb
in fierce, remote villages
are pledging their blood
to borders and funerals.

Men with shoes laced
right up to their knees
are reciting national poems
in trembling voices.

Men of integrity, men
of passion, men with
hatreds notched in bone
are swearing allegiance

to traditional weapons,
the fallen dead,
costume, beverage,
bagpipes and shortbread.

Cooking Rice By The Delia Smith Method

You rinse the grains in three or four washes
of tap water until the water runs clear;
she will be lighting the tea candles
and suspending them in tiny red bowls;
mix water to rice in a ratio of two to one
while she unfurls thick, eclipsing drapery
to block out Scotmid and the bright sunlight;
place the pot on the hob and set your gas
to the thinnest ring of blue you can manage;
from the red velvet bag she will extract
one condom and place it on the bedside table;
now let the rice bubble in its minimal simmer,
and respond to her call from the bedroom
where you will find her laid out on the bed,
having removed, in an obliging gesture,
some of her more hampering articles of dress;
her odours will have sharpened, her mind
will have started to make its crossing
over into that other realm of behaviours
not covered in Delia's cookery manuals;
you will help to finish what she has begun;
in exactly twenty minutes, requiring no further
stirring, touching or intervention of any kind,
the rice will have softened and be ready to eat.

Dog Dinners

Our ancestors started eating meat
before their souls had progressed far enough
to entertain scruples of fellow-feeling.
By the time such powers entered
their delectable brains it was too late:
a lust for animal matter in all its forms
had taken root and rooted deep.

No good lamenting the extremer fringes
of our appetites now – frogs, cats,
guinea pigs, horses, monkeys, other
(beg pardon) human beings – the distinctions
are academic, once the eating begins;
that chicken just fell off its bones;
that was the freshest dog I've ever tasted.

We live until we're eaten – chewed
alive by crashed motor cars or cooked
slowly by patient, methodical diseases;
one dog may be another dog's dinner;
let us compose fine, melodious graces;
starch the table cloths; choose a light, white
wine to serve with the collie. Bon appetit.

Audience Coughing, Bayreuth 1951

Von Karajan is conducting the first
postwar performance of *Die Meistersinger*.
The Festspielhaus smells of Jeyes Fluid –
it has stopped smelling of Hitler by now.
A German audience has crawled out
of the wartime smithereens to listen.

They are in poor health, at the mercy
of colds, infections and parasites,
sorry figures out of Brecht or Otto Dix.
And their coughing has been recorded –
uncontrollable hacking and honking
preserved forever on the master tape.

Their weedy, narrow-chested bodies
haven't fully recovered from a diet
of army belts and floorboards.
Their mouths can still taste rat.
They sit in the dark auditorium
fingering long velvet wounds.

And in the quiet parts they cough.
Their bodies bark with loud contractions.
Their lungs are trying to cough out
war, bomb-dust, rubble and the deaths,
the many deaths they find so hard
to evacuate from their memories.

Duzi Marathon

Balancing dead-weights of water
on their heads, women troop
from that river which ordains,
governs, executes and feeds
a subject people kneeling and working
beside it – furrowing its banks,
driving congregations of cattle
to the communion of its waters,
leading its greatness, in trickles,
to the resuscitation of sickly plants.

Then one day six high-tech racing
canoes come sculling straight through
a thousand years of grinding peasant
subsistence, powered by six laughing
athletes with wrap-around eye-shades,
sports chronometers marvellously
intricate & gadgety as star-ships,
splashing, hollering & hooting
on the foamy back of their toy,
then rounding a bend & vanishing.

Is it any wonder that, next year,
stone-carrying villagers
will be waiting in the reeds?

A Posthumous Dictation
(from Giovanni Jacopo)

In the teeth of admonishing literatures,
despite the opprobrium of decent men
and the furious tut-tutting of the just,
I persist in celebrating your genetically
complicit body, its blessed indecencies,
barefaced inventions concocted for joy.

There isn't time to lull your parents,
swap CVs, colour match our politics,
find out the persuasions of your God,
or follow the long and winding road
of dinners and concerts, with leisure
to swirl and sniff you like a wine buff.

Time only, in the forced proximity
of the poolside shower, to admire obliquely
the ship and shape of you, your perfect
leaps and bounds, inlets and promontories
calculated to a T: an erogenous shoreline
keyed somehow to my deepest inklings.

Skin

A patch of her considered in isolation
(like a section of skin visible through
the green cotton window of a surgical gown)
snaps me awake with its surprising loveliness:

a sub-set of her bodily volumes revealed
in a series of cylindrical amazements,
a gradualness of supplanting planes obeying
the subtlest laws in all of mathematics:

elsewhere an impossible-delicate pallor
inviting the lexicons of snow languages:
absolute Barbarian white giving way to
a courtesan's magnolia sullied by pink;

her colours deepening towards maturity,
darkening into pudendal browns or purples,
the shades of those moist, alluring valves
scribbled over ecstatically with body-hair.

Under Your Skin

On bones these perfections grew and grew
over eighteen, twenty years, achieving
the dropped counterweights of adulthood.

Obstetric glands have ripened inside you
like melons and figs, heavy and sweet,
steeped in plasmas, nectars, syrups.

Like mangoes, like heart-sized avocados,
the pomegranate organs of your gender
lie bedded deep and sound within you,

as heavy as engine parts in the breast
of a motorbike, as large as batteries,
with the density of magnets and dynamos,

from where your gender flowers outwards,
erupting onto the surface of your body
with the powerful blossoms of sex.

Metatarsus Varies

Today you let me touch your swollen foot,
puffy and tender at the base of the toes –
that old condition of yours flaring up.
It was hard to squeeze the shoe back on
so you let me help by doing up the strap,
leaning across you casually and intimately,
sharing thereby a wry acknowledgement
of our midlife's stiffness and stoutness,
though sternly forbidden to stroke your ankle!
There was as much in those secret permissions
hidden from the eyes of nearby colleagues
as complete nakedness, unbridled passion:
your slipped-off shoe, my pitying touches,
discreetly in the crowded coffee lounge.

Darwin's Music

Normally hostile matter relents
under special circumstances
and all necessary biological
fusings and constructions occur
during that unique amnesty:
relationships flourish in the brief
ceasefire, which may show itself as
a secret mutation by moonlight
readying and relaxing some biology:
it turns lilac, or develops a region
of tenderness on its skin
where affinities can take place
and dockings or catalytic touchings –
a fellow of the species will need
to flap by in erratic flight
as if boxed about by biffs of air,
and then sure as chemical destiny
they'll dance to the music
of Darwin, followed by whatever
awkward keyhole surgery
the sexual act takes the form of
in their philosophy.

Historic Computing Machines

The curators know their Operating Systems,
not in the way that deeply reserved Plains Indians

know the old songs and remedies, but as college kids
know Ancient Sumerian or Rocketry in the Third Reich.

Every morning during the popular demonstration hour
they sit in front of primitive, stop-driven consoles

to run vintage Company Accounts, Stock Updates
and Payroll jobs through their classic machines.

They man their room-sized IBM's like aircraft crews
doing practice runs in Heinkels and Lancasters:

museum navigators, co-pilots and rear gunners
drilled in a period aeronautics of props and chocks.

The thoughts are slow; the cloudy valves are blue
and cataracted; insulation peels from tired wiring;

but the registers tally, the gates divide and divert,
ancient programming languages flow in the circuitry.

I hope there'll always be guardians of heritage skills
like these – stone masons, riders of the pennyfarthing,

speakers of Latin keeping Virgil and Ovid sweet,
turning the soil of thousand year old hexameters.

1789

There's a sort of crab that Nature
in her infinite wisdom has moulded
into a monstrous beautiful coral dweller
with a kind of fishing net
in place of a claw, a gentrified pincer
with frond-shaped webbing
that springs open like a Spanish fan
as fast blinking to sift and sieve
the clouds of rich microscopic muck
that pour off the fertile coral beds.
If Darwin's right, a thousand years
of unbroken lineage in the crab
was needed to make the French lace
of this clever, delicate scoop,
its membrane finer than gauze
and all part of a faultless marine machine
that works perfectly every time
so it seems such a pity to see it get
taken, crushed and consumed
after one powerful, punching lunge
by a long, grey, hard-nosed eel.

Sound Engineer

She runs the magnetic spool backwards
and forwards to identify ugly glottal lumps
in the vocal tissue; finds one, snips it out
and neatly closes the gap: a noisy swallow
lies on the floor on one inch of recording –

a language beautician is at work, cutting
gristly blurts and mishaps from my delivery.
I listen in amazement as she isolates
a sigh, removes and transfers this tiny
puff – intact – into a different utterance.

She directs her art to linguistic particles,
splicing morphemes and phonemes
like someone transplanting a cornea.
She's a word surgeon, widening vowels
or punching tracheotomies into sentences.

I end up speaking like an angel, in a purified
dialect free from acoustic transgressions,
while around her feet, on snippets of tape,
inarticulate phonic fragments of my voice
continue to gulp and hiss and croak.

Powers Over There

The pure sheet of intellection warps
and twists as it gets further away from us;
it cannot hold steady our vision
of how things, by basic common sense,
must be – the world of decent reason.

Once our flimsy constructs fall into
such gravities and compressions, such
tractions and air intensities, integrity
in the material goes; barometric forces
of ethnicity crumple their air frames,

distant mythologies exercise the strength
of their local irrationalities and ties;
even simple family life, with its pudding-
bowl haircuts, ugg boots and fedoras,
puts a strain on the frail membrane.

Belief travels poorly through languages,
hobbling over participles and gerunds.
Sectarian ideas creep in, and wrinkle
the texture, as water buckles paper.
Faith sweeps minds with hurricane force.

Extinction Level Events

I'm being showered by oblivion, sprayed
by pellets of anaesthesia and paralysis.
Everyday life is driving extinction into me,
sinking slugs of numbness and morbidity.

They stiffen the visceral technology of me,
thicken and thug the delicate
springworks of life that tremble with balance
and precision in hair-fine mechanisms.

Days are turning my intricacies coarse
and leathery and a whisker away
from seizure and total cessation.
I can't get out of this bombardment.

Isolation

Heartbeats travel down my elbows
onto a rigid table top that skids them
into a bottle of carbonated water
where they continue to throb;
they send quivers across the liquid
like the pulsings of a jellyfish.

White as a bloodless heart
the jellyfish travels with a cardiac
rhythm, an organ without a body,
squeezing itself through coronary seas;
in the absence of blood
it pumps its own movement.

My heart's waves are diverted to
an aortic pump that loops the blood
along tubes and cleans it with drugs
before returning it to my body;
my blood hangs in space like
an astronaut floating alongside his craft.

I am distributed into my closest
surroundings, carried by sounds
and silent thumpings into physical spaces
outside my biological self;
I breathe into plants, I bleed into
machines. I form part of the world.

The Fierce Wheat In Samuel Palmer

Every day falls open at the right place,
spread full and flat like a heavy journal.
Rook pairs stand perfectly modelled in fields
tilted at roof angles. Yellow broom signals
the abiding of Albion and of rare Jerusalem
in successions of plant life and summer air.
Each day offers room for achieving things in,
but what? Obviously, like Garibaldi,
you can land on the divided Italian coast,
your snaking, pike-haired columns making
a strong impression on even a very large day.
But those are career moves, don't explain
why beautiful, eye-leaved Egyptian bushes
waylay us with unnecessary abundance.

Labours Of Delight

If trees could experience things
this one would feel wonderful.
All that new material bursting
from swollen tips would make it
tingle with tightness and pressure
all over its boundaries.

The first poke of feathery growth
would tickle and provoke;
casings would split to show
tufts of blossom like lacy
edges of luxurious underwear,
and be full of prickly sensation.

The whole tree hums with attention,
at every point developments
are stretching the botanic bounds
to make something new, increasing
the tree's awareness of itself,
making it seem more alive.

In fact it is more alive. Buds throb
like teasingly painful fingertips,
nature's tough love brings it
to the peak of consciousness,
multiplies sweet birthing agonies
over the whole of its prolific crown.

Quiet Reading Room

A small river of noises
crackles through the silence,
a thin stream of ticking,
tapping, like snapping grass,
a current of little sounds –
this is the voice of study;

the body does not ponder
noiselessly, with the deep
stillness of abstraction itself;
the thinking machine is
a moist material being
with fidgetty motor appendages,

hands roving compulsively
over books, pencil cases,
keyboards and glug-bottles,
from whence that trickle
of rattles and clatters:
the sinewy rustle of thought.

Why I Am Not A Poet

Because he was a white collar artist himself
Rilke envied those of a much earthier mould,
the manual labourers in clay, pigment or stone.
He admired the pugilistic hands of a sculptor,
big and knuckly, but gentle as a grandmother's.

How gratifying to know that your art materials
were wrenched with jack-hammers and dynamite
off the face of a cliff, trucked all the way
from Brittany to Paris, then lifted by crane, with much
effing and blinding, onto your studio floor.

Wouldn't it be great to get up at 10 on a weekday
and head off downriver with some food, an extra jersey
and all the tricks of your trade in one grimy box.
Then line up your easel like a quantity surveyor
and start mapping steeples, bridges and willows.

Before long, you've drawn a small, admiring crowd,
then it's just dab, dab, dab until you're all done.
Back home, you're as tired and happy as a fisherman
with three trout in his bag, and the pretty woman
who followed you back is taking off her clothes for you.

But if you're a poet, you have to stay home, hunched over
a desk, trying to fix invisible problems of language.
Everything beautiful is a distraction – music, windows,
the visible world itself. You squint at sheets of paper,
perplexed, like a minor official correcting an affidavit.

The Daisy In My Wake

A daisy in my *Finnegans Wake*
squashed by the weight of pages
has left a stain on some printed
expressions of paper and ink
but its brown sap and odour
have not entered language itself;
language is airless and odourless,
it does not occupy any space,
there is nowhere for the world
to enter and leave a mark;
words can be pulled out of shape
by the massive continental magnets
of a million native speakers,
by the lobbying of entire civil-
izations of speech communities,
but take no moisture or fragrance
from tiny dry petals of a flower
picked on Howth Head in 1982.

In A Hide

Only when my body has powered off
its auxiliary systems, and stopped
chewing, shuffling, sniffing & scratching
until all it does is breathe and attend –
only then does language drift back to me
in single words, followed by wedded pairs,
then whole grammatical flights of them
like the return of scared-off birds,
the trickle-back of shy ground-animals,
until confident populations of sound
settle full-voiced over the area
and flowerless trees fill with the squeals
of a hundred, tiny, rusted wheels.